Kindergarten Homework

Real-Life Activities that Turn Homework into Family Fun

Written by Debbie Martinez

Illustrated by Ann Iosa

Edited by Mary Pat Ferraro and Sue Lewis

Project Directed by Carolea Williams

D1609107

Table of Contents

Introduction

Homework in Kindergarten? Why?

As children enter kindergarten, they are eager and ready to learn. And these enthusiastic young students enjoy age-appropriate homework with assignments that provide successful learning experiences. When kindergarten homework is fun and meaningful, it lays the foundation for good work habits in later years. Furthermore, positive homework or homeplay helps establish the home-school connection and involves parents as partners in their child's daily learning experiences.

The Real-Life Kindergarten Homework Book

- includes creative activities that transform homework into "homeplay"—a positive, exciting, and creative experience for early learners.

- provides ready-to-go reproducibles requiring almost no teacher preparation time.

- gives the whole family the opportunity to be part of the homework process.

- empowers parents with information and practical ideas they can easily implement as they become partners in their child's education.

- describes techniques for parents to help their children establish the good work habits essential for successful learning.

- offers teachers a choice in how to present homework to their students, giving them flexibility to tailor the methods to meet their students' needs.

Types of Homework Activities

Design your own homework program by choosing from the following types of activities included in *Kindergarten Homework*.

Monthly Calendars
Twelve monthly calendars with five learning activities per week are provided. Parents and children can complete a specific number of activities each week and then complete a response journal designed for the month. A blank calendar is also provided so you can design your own activities.

Monthly Celebrations
Two activities following a seasonal theme are provided for each month of the year. Parents and students can complete one of the monthly celebrations and then return a record of the celebration to school.

Alphabet Fun
These entertaining alphabet activities are easy to use. Each activity includes a story about several letters and a list of possible activities. Parents and children can complete the activities and return a work sample from the many choices listed for each activity to school.

Across the Curriculum
Simple, engaging homework activities are presented for language arts, math, science, music, art, and physical education. A short introduction tells why each activity is important, and simple directions lead children and parents through each step. Send these activities home to correlate with a current topic of study or a thematic unit.

Family Adventures
Family adventures are designed for students and their entire families to enjoy. Families are invited to experience both real and imaginary adventures. Several suggestions are offered for each activity so children and parents can choose how they will complete the homework.

Timely Tips Newsletters
These reproducible newsletters provide parents with information to help make their child's learning experience at home even more productive. Topics include homework tips, reading, television-viewing, learning on the go, and building a child's self-confidence. Send the newsletters home throughout the year with your regular classroom newsletter to keep parents informed.

Monthly Calendars

Monthly Calendars provide real-life activity ideas for parents to do with their children. Many take only minutes to do and require easy-to-find items from around the house.

To begin, fill in the number of activities you expect students to complete each week. Duplicate the calendar and the response journal page for the month; staple them together for each child. Send them home on the first school day of each month.

Ask students to return their calendars and response journals on the last school day of the month. After you receive them, review the response journals to evaluate which activities you'd like to include in future plans.

A blank calendar at the end of this section invites you to customize a month-full of learning to meet your students' needs. You might even want to create a month's calendar of activities for a particular child or group of children.

The July and August calendars can be used for summer homework or for year-round schools.

Name _____

Choose at least _____ activities to complete each week. Check the box in the lower right corner of each calendar square as your child completes the activity. Turn in the calendar and the response journal on the last school day of September.

September

Monday	Tuesday	Wednesday	Thursday	Friday
Pretend you have a magic pencil box at school. What is inside? How is it magic?	Place paper over a fallen leaf, and rub over it with the flat side of a crayon.	Draw a picture of your teacher. Name three things you like about your teacher.	Finish this sentence: *One thing I want to learn this year is . . .*	Point to all the words that start with the letter *B* on a book page.
Tell the name of your school.	Name two things you do every day in school.	Make a pattern using leaves.	Name two words that rhyme with *tree*.	Hop, skip, kneel, jog, and twist ten times each.
Name five people in your class.	Gather ten leaves from the ground. Group them by color or shape.	Write your first name.	Write your phone number.	Count all the cans of food in your cupboard.
Name five different foods made from apples.	Write the alphabet in capital letters.	Help prepare dinner.	Say your address.	Draw a picture of yourself and what you hear, smell, see, touch, and taste.
Practice introducing yourself to your classmates.	Have someone read a story to you. Retell the story in your own words.	Write the numbers from 0 to 10.	Look at all the pictures in a book before someone reads it to you.	Say ten words that start with the sound *s*.

September Response Journal

Help your child dictate responses as you write them down. Turn in this journal along with the calendar on the last school day of September.

Child

1. My favorite activity was _____ .

   I liked it because _____

   _____ .

2. One activity I needed help with was _____

   _____ .

3. I learned _____

   _____ .

Parent

1. I learned _____ .

2. The activity I most enjoyed doing with my child was _____

   _____ .

3. The activity I helped my child with most was _____

   _____ .

Parent's Signature _____

Name _____

Choose at least _____ activities to complete each week. Check the box in the lower right corner of each calendar square as your child completes the activity. Turn in the calendar and the response journal on the last school day of October.

October

Monday	Tuesday	Wednesday	Thursday	Friday
If you could be an animal, what would you be and why?	Make up a story about a scary pumpkin patch.	Tell the story to your family.	Write the name of a grandparent.	Recite the nursery rhyme "Little Miss Muffet." Would you have run away?
Do something special for someone in your family.	List ten things in your classroom.	Using a string, measure around a pumpkin and then around your waist. Which is bigger?	Do ten jumping jacks, ten sit-ups, and ten knee bends.	Have someone read a story to you. Predict how it will end before the last page.
Finish this sentence: *I like fall because . . .*	Hold ten pennies in one hand and ten rice grains in the other. Which weighs more?	Dry out some pumpkin seeds. Glue the seeds to paper to make a picture.	Draw a picture with a pumpkin, a bat, and the moon in it.	Say the sounds for letters A to M.
Have someone read a story to you. Tell what you would do if you were in the story.	Tell someone five ways people can travel.	Name ten words that start with P.	Count your steps from the kitchen to the front door. Have an adult do the same. Who took more steps?	Draw a picture of yourself in a favorite costume.
Say the names of all the people in your family.	Which melts faster, an ice cube or a scoop of ice cream? Try it!	Write the alphabet in lowercase letters.	Name all the words you can that rhyme with *bat*.	Tell three safety tips for trick-or-treating on Halloween.

October Response Journal

Help your child dictate responses as you write them down. Turn in this journal along with the calendar on the last school day of October.

Child

1. My favorite activity was _____ .

   I liked it because _____

   _____ .

2. One activity I needed help with was _____

   _____ .

3. I learned _____

   _____ .

Parent

1. I learned _____ .

2. The activity I most enjoyed doing with my child was _____

   _____ .

3. The activity I helped my child with most was _____

   _____ .

Parent's Signature _____

Name _____

Choose at least _____ activities to complete each week. Check the box in the lower right corner of each calendar square as your child completes the activity. Turn in the calendar and the response journal on the last school day of November.

 # November

Monday	Tuesday	Wednesday	Thursday	Friday
Tell five things you like to do with your family in the fall.	Name all the words you can that start with the letter *N*.	Point to all the words that end with the letter *T* on a book page.	Tell what you think it would have been like to travel on the *Mayflower*.	Measure five things in your house. Which is the shortest? Longest?
What famous person would you like to meet and what would you say to this person?	Make up and tell a story about five little pilgrims and a turkey.	Make popcorn. Glue the kernels onto paper to write the letters in your name.	Say your address.	If you could invite any person to Thanksgiving dinner, who would it be? Why?
Guess how long it will take you to get dressed. Then have a family member time you.	Trace around your hand. Then draw a turkey from the tracing.	Guess how long it will take for an ice cube to melt. Time it to check your guess.	Finish this sentence: *I am thankful for* _____ *because . . .*	Look at a clock. What hour is it?
Write your last name. Iosa	Write a friend's phone number.	Name the foods your family will eat on Thanksgiving Day.	Have someone help you write and attach labels to objects in your bedroom.	Say the numbers from 0 to 20.
Make a pattern of sounds by clapping and snapping. Have someone copy you.	If you were principal of your school, what rule would you make? Why?	If you could give a gift to another family on Thanksgiving Day, what would it be?	Design a bookmark for the month of November.	Do something special for someone in your family.

10

November Response Journal

Help your child dictate responses as you write them down. Turn in this journal along with the calendar on the last school day of November.

Child

1. My favorite activity was _____ .

   I liked it because _____

   _____ .

2. One activity I needed help with was _____

   _____ .

3. I learned _____

   _____ .

Parent

1. I learned _____ .

2. The activity I most enjoyed doing with my child was _____

   _____ .

3. The activity I helped my child with most was _____

   _____ .

Parent's Signature _____

Name _____

Choose at least _____ activities to complete each week. Check the box in the lower right corner of each calendar square as your child completes the activity. Turn in the calendar and the response journal on the last school day of December.

 # December

Monday	Tuesday	Wednesday	Thursday	Friday
Draw a picture of your family ice-skating.	Tell a story about five snowmen and five children.	Read about a menorah. Tell someone what it is.	Sing a favorite winter celebration song.	Draw a picture of your whole body and label important parts.
Put on at least four winter clothing items.	Think of an imaginary pet. What would it do? Act it out.	Read about Christmas trees. Tell why people put them in their houses.	Write your address.	Have someone read *The Gingerbread Man* to you.
Make wrapping paper by dipping cookie cutters into paint and pressing them on paper.	Name three animals that like cold weather.	Do 15 jumping jacks. Ask an adult to do them with you.	Name five things you like about your best friend.	Make a wish for the coming year.
Name all the things that remind you of your favorite winter celebration.	Finish this sentence: *If I could give all the children in the world a gift, my gift would be . . .*	Draw a picture of five penguins. How many eyes do they have altogether?	Write your name vertically. Write a word that starts with each letter of your name.	Plan a New Year's Eve party just for kids.
If you could have one gift, what would it be? Why?	Make hot chocolate with an adult.	Write a thank-you note to someone who gave you a gift.	If you could be a toy, which one would you be? Why?	Finish this sentence: *This year was great because . . .*

December Response Journal

Help your child dictate responses as you write them down. Turn in this journal along with the calendar on the last school day of December.

Child

1. My favorite activity was _____.

   I liked it because _____

   _____.

2. One activity I needed help with was _____

   _____.

3. I learned _____

   _____.

Parent

1. I learned _____.

2. The activity I most enjoyed doing with my child was _____

   _____.

3. The activity I helped my child with most was _____

   _____.

Parent's Signature _____

Name _____

Choose at least _____ activities to complete each week. Check the box in the lower right corner of each calendar square as your child completes the activity. Turn in the calendar and the response journal on the last school day of January.

January

Monday	Tuesday	Wednesday	Thursday	Friday
Make a New Year's resolution.	Write the numbers from 0 to 10. *0123456*	Draw a winter picture using a triangle, a circle, a square, and a rectangle.	Say the sound each letter of the alphabet makes.	Say the days of the week.
Say your first, middle, and last names.	Look at a clock's hands. To which numbers are they pointing?	Count your steps as you walk from your bedroom to the kitchen.	Which is less? 3 or 5? 10 or 6? 7 or 8?	Make the letter J into a silly January picture.
Open a book to any page. Point to the words that start with the letter J.	Write your first name.	Say the alphabet.	Help someone fix dinner.	Write the name of someone in your family.
Write your age on a piece of paper.	Count the beds in your house.	Name ten things bigger than a chair.	Write the alphabet from A to K in capital and lowercase letters.	Talk about Martin Luther King. What is a dream that you have?
Put your hand *above*, *behind*, and *under* a chair. Say the word as you do it.	Call a friend on the telephone.	Think of three words that rhyme with *snow*.	Count all the pieces of furniture in the living room.	Say the opposite of each word: *day, hot, big, sad, long, up,* and *over*.

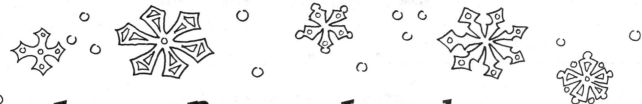

January Response Journal

Help your child dictate responses as you write them down. Turn in this journal along with the calendar on the last school day of January.

Child

1. My favorite activity was _____ .

   I liked it because _____

   _____ .

2. One activity I needed help with was _____

   _____ .

3. I learned _____

   _____ .

Parent

1. I learned _____ .

2. The activity I most enjoyed doing with my child was _____

   _____ .

3. The activity I helped my child with most was _____

   _____ .

Parent's Signature _____

Name _____

Choose at least _____ activities to complete each week. Check the box in the lower right corner of each calendar square as your child completes the activity. Turn in the calendar and the response journal on the last school day of February.

February

Monday	Tuesday	Wednesday	Thursday	Friday
Name ten things that start with the letter *F*.	Point to and say the days of the week on this calendar. Which days are missing?	Look at Lincoln's picture on a penny. Have someone read the words printed on the penny to you.	Copy the word *February*.	Do five sit-ups.
Write the alphabet from *L* to *Z* in capital and lowercase letters.	Lace a pair of shoes.	Look at Washington's picture on a dollar. Have someone read the words printed on the dollar to you.	Cut out a heart shape.	Stand on one foot for 20 seconds. Then switch feet.
Draw a picture of your home.	Write the numbers from 0 to 20.	Make a Valentine for someone.	Name ten things smaller than a shoe box.	Which is more? 12 or 14? 16 or 20? 5 or 7?
Have someone read *The Three Bears* or tell you the story.	Make your bed and one other bed.	Do ten jumping jacks.	Say the sound each letter of the alphabet makes.	Bounce a ball with one hand five times.
Act out *The Three Bears*.	Write your name and a friend's name.	Count the stairs in or near your house.	Make the letter *F* into a silly February picture.	Write the names of everyone in your family.

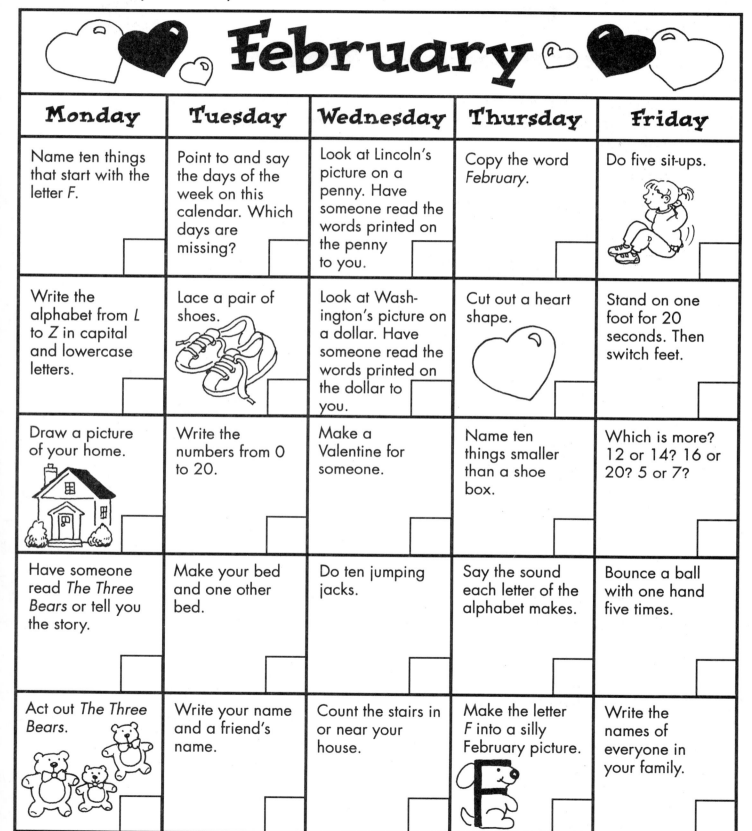

February Response Journal

Help your child dictate responses as you write them down. Turn in this journal along with the calendar on the last school day of February.

Child

1. My favorite activity was _____.

   I liked it because _____

   _____ .

2. One activity I needed help with was _____

   _____ .

3. I learned _____

   _____ .

Parent

1. I learned _____ .

2. The activity I most enjoyed doing with my child was _____

   _____ .

3. The activity I helped my child with most was _____

   _____ .

Parent's Signature _____

 Creative Teaching Press, Inc.

Choose at least _____ activities to complete each week. Check the box in the lower right corner of each calendar square as your child completes the activity. Turn in the calendar and the response journal on the last school day of March.

 # March

Monday	Tuesday	Wednesday	Thursday	Friday
Draw five things you can find in the sky.	Say the days of the week.	Set the table. Count the forks, spoons, and knives.	Trace around a plastic lid. Make a design from the tracing.	Zip and unzip a a jacket ten times. Count as you zip.
Tell the opposites of *wet*, *boy*, *left*, *down*, *happy*, *fat*, *open*, and *tall*.	Point to your left hand; point to your right hand.	Put your hand *over*, *under*, *behind*, and *beside* a table.	Name ten things larger than a television set.	Tell someone what you would do if you found a pot of gold.
Listen to a story and draw your favorite part.	Find all the round shapes in a room in your house.	Point to the letters *A*, *F*, and *T* on a book page.	Write the numbers from 0 to 20.	What day is today? What day will tomorrow be?
Draw a rainbow with red, orange, yellow, green, blue, and purple stripes.	Write a parent's work phone number.	Name two words that rhyme with *ran*.	Make a St. Patrick's Day card for a family member.	Count your jumps aloud as you jump from your bed to the bathroom.
Write the ages of all the people in your family. Don't forget yourself!	Write the alphabet in lowercase letters.	Add up the number of toes in your family.	Go outside and listen for one minute. Name all the sounds you hear.	Make a sandwich. Cut it into two equal pieces.

Name _____

March Response Journal

Help your child dictate responses as you write them down. Turn in this journal along with the calendar on the last school day of March.

Child

1. My favorite activity was _____ .

   I liked it because _____

   _____ .

2. One activity I needed help with was _____

   _____ .

3. I learned _____

   _____ .

Parent

1. I learned _____ .

2. The activity I most enjoyed doing with my child was _____

   _____ .

3. The activity I helped my child with most was _____

   _____ .

Parent's Signature _____

Name _____

Choose at least _____ activities to complete each week. Check the box in the lower right corner of each calendar square as your child completes the activity. Turn in the calendar and the response journal on the last school day of April.

 # April

Monday	Tuesday	Wednesday	Thursday	Friday
Tell someone a make-believe story about a raindrop.	Write the alphabet in capital letters.	Finish this sentence: *The world would be a better place if everyone . . .*	Pretend you are a raindrop floating to the ground. Act it out.	Look at a clock. Name the minute.
List five words that describe you.	Make happy, sad, scared, angry, and excited faces.	Retell your favorite story to someone in your family.	Bounce a ball five times with one hand and then the other.	Guess how many spoonfuls of rice it takes to fill a glass. Try it.
Draw a picture of what you want to be when you grow up.	Have someone read you a story. Change the ending.	Write your name five times, each time with a different crayon.	Write the numbers from 15 to 30.	Put a handful of toothpicks or pennies into groups of ten. How many groups do you have?
Write your phone number.	Say the sound of each letter in the alphabet.	Read a book to a family member by describing the pictures.	Measure the people in your family. Who is the tallest? Shortest?	Fill a tray with sand or rice. With your finger, write the numbers from 1 to 10 in the tray.
Draw a picture of what you and your best friend like to do together.	Find all the square shapes in one room of your house.	Draw a picture of your favorite animal.	Fill a cup half-full with water.	Name ten things bigger than a car.

April Response Journal

Help your child dictate responses as you write them down. Turn in this journal along with the calendar on the last school day of April.

Child

1. My favorite activity was _____ .

   I liked it because _____

   _____ .

2. One activity I needed help with was _____

   _____ .

3. I learned _____

   _____ .

Parent

1. I learned _____ .

2. The activity I most enjoyed doing with my child was _____

   _____ .

3. The activity I helped my child with most was _____

   _____ .

Parent's Signature _____

Name _____

Choose at least _____ activities to complete each week. Check the box in the lower right corner of each calendar square as your child completes the activity. Turn in the calendar and the response journal on the last school day of May.

May

Monday	Tuesday	Wednesday	Thursday	Friday
If you were king or queen of the world, what would you do first?	Tell a story about five angry bees. Draw a picture of the story.	Point to and say the first and the last letters of each word on a book page.	Trace around one of your feet. Make a silly picture from the tracing.	Design a flag that tells about you. Happy Likes School
Hop from your kitchen to the front door. Count each hop aloud.	Cut out a flower shape.	Set the table. Count the forks and knives.	Name as many things as you can that start with the sound k.	Name your favorite springtime sport.
Write your first and last names.	Write the names of the people in your family.	Tell one way that spring is different from winter.	List five words that rhyme with May.	List five things that make you happy.
Pantomime working in an ice-cream shop. Have someone guess what you are doing.	Name five items made from wood.	Compliment a family member.	Name your favorite picnic food. Draw a picture of it.	Finish this sentence: If I could teach everyone in the world one thing . . .
Give someone directions on how to walk from your bedroom to the kitchen.	Name five items made from plastic.	Use spoons and forks to make a pattern.	Do something special for a neighbor.	Write the numbers from 20 to 40.

May Response Journal

Help your child dictate responses as you write them down. Turn in this journal along with the calendar on the last school day of May.

Child

1. My favorite activity was _____ .

   I liked it because _____

   _____ .

2. One activity I needed help with was _____

   _____ .

3. I learned _____

   _____ .

Parent

1. I learned _____ .

2. The activity I most enjoyed doing with my child was _____

   _____ .

3. The activity I helped my child with most was _____

   _____ .

Parent's Signature _____

Name _____

Choose at least _____ activities to complete each week. Check the box in the lower right corner of each calendar square as your child completes the activity. Turn in the calendar and the response journal on the last school day of June.

June

Monday	Tuesday	Wednesday	Thursday	Friday
Close your eyes and listen for one minute. Draw a picture of different things you heard.	Count the windows in your home.	Name three words that rhyme with *June*.	List four things taller than your house.	Which weighs more, a handful of raisins or a handful of cereal? Try it!
Say the days of the week.	Write the numbers from 30 to 50.	Do five sit-ups. Do ten jumping jacks.	Cut a magazine picture into several pieces. Put the puzzle back together.	Write the names of five animals that live in a forest.
Tell a funny story about a day at the beach.	Draw a picture using a circle, a square, a triangle, a rectangle, an oval, and a diamond.	List all the farm animals you can.	Say your address two times.	Jump over a crack in the sidewalk five times.
Write your first and last names.	Read a book to someone by describing the pictures.	Write your telephone number.	Name ten things smaller than you.	Make a sandwich. Cut it in half, then in fourths.
Write the names of five friends.	If you could travel anywhere in the world, where would it be? Why?	Write a friend's telephone number.	Take a walk outside. Collect ten objects and make a design from them.	Say the months of the year.

June Response Journal

Help your child dictate responses as you write them down. Turn in this journal along with the calendar on the last school day of June.

Child

1. My favorite activity was _____ .

   I liked it because _____

   _____ .

2. One activity I needed help with was _____

   _____ .

3. I learned _____

   _____ .

Parent

1. I learned _____ .

2. The activity I most enjoyed doing with my child was _____

   _____ .

3. The activity I helped my child with most was _____

   _____ .

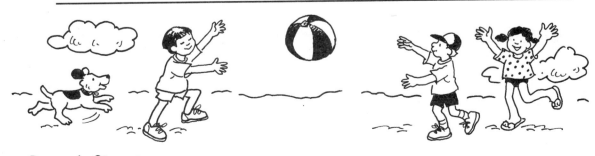

Parent's Signature _____

Name _____

Choose at least _____ activities to complete each week. Check the box in the lower right corner of each calendar square as your child completes the activity. Turn in the calendar and the response journal on the last school day of July.

July

Monday	Tuesday	Wednesday	Thursday	Friday
Show the numbers from 1 to 10 using popcorn.	Point to your right ankle; point to your left knee.	Go for a walk. Then draw a picture of five things you remember seeing.	Do ten knee bends and ten jumping jacks.	Draw a picture of a garden.
Trace around your foot and a grown-up's foot. Make a silly picture from the tracings.	Which is less? 10 or 20? 15 or 18? 8 or 4?	Write the alphabet in capital and lowercase letters.	Name five ways to cool off on a hot day.	Do something nice for someone in your family.
Write your first and last names.	Set the table. Count the total number of items on the table.	Help someone make dinner.	Tell someone five words that start with the letter S.	Say the numbers from 1 to 5 by their ordinal names (first, second . . .).
Tell someone a story about a Fourth of July adventure.	Copy the word July. Then draw a picture of the American flag.	Go outside and count the steps you take from one end of your home to the other.	Unlace and then lace your shoes.	Count by fives to 25.
If you were President of the United States, what would you do first?	Have someone read a story to you. Tell a different ending for the story.	Say the days of the week.	Finish this sentence: I like my best friend because . . .	Name five healthful foods.

July Response Journal

Help your child dictate responses as you write them down. Turn in this journal along with the calendar on the last school day of July.

Child

1. My favorite activity was _____.

   I liked it because _____

   _____.

2. One activity I needed help with was _____

   _____.

3. I learned _____

   _____.

Parent

1. I learned _____.

2. The activity I most enjoyed doing with my child was _____

   _____.

3. The activity I helped my child with most was _____

   _____.

Parent's Signature _____

Name _____

Choose at least _____ activities to complete each week. Check the box in the lower right corner of each calendar square as your child completes the activity. Turn in the calendar and the response journal on the last school day of August.

August

Monday	Tuesday	Wednesday	Thursday	Friday
Name five living things. Name five nonliving things.	Sing one of your favorite songs out loud.	Look at a clock. What hour is it?	Balance on one foot as long as you can. Then balance on the other foot.	Finish this sentence: *My family is important because . . .*
Write the numbers as far as you can go. Stop if you get to 100!	Jog in place for two minutes. Is your heart pumping quickly?	Name five ocean animals.	Put a book on your head. Walk across the room without dropping the book.	Make three wishes and draw a picture of one.
Write a thank-you note to someone who did something nice for you.	Count all the lamps in your home.	Say the months of the year.	Tell someone five things you like about yourself.	Write the alphabet in capital and lowercase letters.
Name the four seasons. Draw a summer picture.	Write a list of five things to do in the summer.	Count the total number of fingers and eyes on people in your house.	Draw a picture of a picnic basket and the items you would put in it.	Pretend you are going camping. Tell someone all the things you would take.
Say the sound of each letter in the alphabet.	Cut a magazine picture into several pieces. Put the puzzle back together.	Lay a rope on the floor. Walk forward and backward next to it.	Tell someone a story about a fish who couldn't be caught.	Recite the nursery rhyme "Jack and Jill."

August Response Journal

Help your child dictate responses as you write them down. Turn in this journal along with the calendar on the last school day of August.

Child

1. My favorite activity was _____ .

    I liked it because _____

    _____ .

2. One activity I needed help with was _____

    _____ .

3. I learned _____

    _____ .

Parent

1. I learned _____ .

2. The activity I most enjoyed doing with my child was _____

    _____ .

3. The activity I helped my child with most was _____

    _____ .

Parent's Signature _____

Name _____

Monday	Tuesday	Wednesday	Thursday	Friday

- -

To the teacher: Use this calendar for any month. Write your own activities.

Monthly Celebrations

Monthly Celebrations homework offers students the opportunity to learn while celebrating seasonal themes and holidays. These easy, fun activities don't take much time, but it's time parents will find well spent with their children.

Send home the Monthly Celebrations homework at the beginning of the month. Tell the children that they may complete the activity anytime during the month. Encourage parents to participate in the learning process with their children.

At the end of each activity students are asked to share their responses at the bottom of the page. The students may write their answers on their own or with help from their parents. Have children return the homework page on the last school day of the month.

You can use the August Homework Celebration for summer homework or in year-round schools. Pick a Celebration on page 44 can be used anytime during the year.

Name _____

The First Day of Fall

Choose one activity. When it is completed, help your child dictate responses as you write them down at the bottom of the page. Return this page on the last school day of September.

1. Fall Collage

Talk with your child about the seasonal changes that occur in fall. Go on a nature walk and gather "fall items" such as acorns, leaves of different colors, twigs, grass, and pine cones. Have your child glue the items on cardboard to make a collage. Display the collage in the house for everyone to admire.

2. Raking Fun

Have your child estimate the number of lawn bags your family will fill with leaves as you rake the yard. Rake the yard together and invite your child to count the bags when you are finished. Discuss your child's estimate compared to the actual number of filled bags.

Tell about the activity you chose. What did you like about it?

_____

_____

_____

Parent's Signature _____

Pumpkin Time

Choose one activity. When it is completed, help your child dictate responses as you write them down at the bottom of the page. Return this page on the last school day of October.

1. Pumpkin Face

Have your child choose a pumpkin to decorate. As a family, use scrap material such as fabric, pipe cleaners, sticks, buttons, and glue to design a silly face for the pumpkin. Have your child dictate a story about the pumpkin as you write it down for him or her. Read the story to the family.

2. Baked Pumpkin Seeds

Cut open a pumpkin and help your child remove the seeds. As a family, complete the following recipe. Invite your child to measure, mix, and stir as you complete the recipe.

Baked Pumpkin Seeds

In a large bowl, mix 2 cups unwashed pumpkin seeds with $\frac{1}{2}$ teaspoon Worcestershire Sauce, 2 tablespoons melted butter, and $1\frac{1}{2}$ teaspoons salt. Spread the seeds on a cookie sheet, and bake for approximately 2 hours in a 250° oven until dry and golden brown. Cool and enjoy!

Tell about the activity you chose. What did you like about it?

_____

_____

_____

Parent's Signature _____

Thanksgiving

Choose one activity. When it is completed, help your child dictate responses as you write them down at the bottom of the page. Return this page on the last school day of November.

1. Thanksgiving Turkey

Have everyone in the family trace around his or her hand on paper and design a turkey from the tracing (the thumb becomes the head). Ask family members to write one thing they are thankful for on each "finger" of the traced hand. Display the turkeys around the house.

2. Giving Back

As a family, spend part of Thanksgiving Day or a day in November at a place that allows you to "give back," such as a nursing home, hospital, or homeless shelter. Visit people who might be lonely on this holiday. Invite your family to share their feelings after the experience.

Tell about the activity you chose. What did you like about it?

_____

_____

_____

Parent's Signature _____

Happy Holidays

Choose one activity. When it is completed, help your child dictate responses as you write them down at the bottom of the page. Return this page on the last school day of December.

1. Holiday Wishes

Ask your child to make a list of five special people. Have your child think of one wish for each person and draw a picture of the wish. Your child can then send the picture to each special person.

I wish Grandma could have a new cat.

2. Favorite Celebration

Discuss as a family your favorite December celebration such as Chanukah, Christmas, or Kwanzaa. Explain the significance of the celebration to the people who celebrate it. Have each family member tell what they like most about the celebration and why it is special to them.

Tell about the activity you chose. What did you like about it?

_____

_____

_____

Parent's Signature _____

The New Year

Choose one activity. When it is completed, help your child dictate responses as you write them down at the bottom of the page. Return this page on the last school day of January.

1. New Year's Thoughts

As a family, make a list of ten things that were special for your family this past year. Then make a list of the things your family hopes will happen this coming year.

Special Things	Hope Will Happen
• We went camping to Yosemite.	• We hope we go to Yellowstone park.
• We got a new kitten.	

2. First Snowman of the Year

During January, go outside as a family and build a snowman. If there isn't any snow, make a snowman from cardboard boxes. Decorate the snowman for all to admire.

Tell about the activity you chose. What did you like about it?

_____

_____

_____

Parent's Signature _____

Valentine's Day

Choose one activity. When it is completed, help your child dictate responses as you write them down at the bottom of the page. Return this page on the last school day of February.

1. List of Love

As a family, talk about important people in your lives. Make a list, and write down reasons each person is important to your family.

Important People

Grandma
    She is important.
    She loves us and
    we love her.
Debbie
    Debbie is our best neighbor.
She watches us when
mom and dad aren't home.

2. Valentine's Day Surprise

Have your child think of people who would like to be surprised with a Valentine's Day card, such as a neighbor, friend, or relative. Invite your child to make a card from art supplies such as paper, doilies, crayons, glue, buttons, glitter, and scissors. If possible, make arrangements for your child to deliver the valentine in person or mail it.

Tell about the activity you chose. What did you like about it?

_____

_____

_____

Parent's Signature _____

St. Patrick's Day

Choose one activity. When it is completed, help your child dictate responses as you write them down at the bottom of the page. Return this page on the last school day of March.

1. Lucky Day

Have a family discussion about why each family member is "lucky" in life. Have your child draw a picture of a rainbow with a pot of gold at the end. Then have your child draw a picture under the rainbow to show why he or she is lucky.

2. St. Patrick's Day Feast

Have your child help you prepare a simple St. Patrick's Day meal of baked potatoes and toppings, such as cheese, tomatoes, chicken pieces, olives, sour cream, avocados, etc.

Tell about the activity you chose. What did you like about it?

_____

_____

_____

Parent's Signature _____

Spring

Choose one activity. When it is completed, help your child dictate responses as you write them down at the bottom of the page. Return this page on the last school day of April.

1. Outside Garden

Talk about gardens and the spring planting season. As a family, visit a local nursery. Invite each family member to choose a flower or vegetable to grow in a garden. Work together to plant and tend the garden. Then enjoy the results!

2. Inside Garden

Discuss how seeds are often planted in the spring. Invite your child to watch a seed grow indoors. Use toothpicks to suspend a sweet potato or an avocado seed in a glass of water. Put the glass near a window for sunlight. In several days your child will see roots beginning to form. Have your child place the plant in a large pot with soil, water the plant regularly, and watch it grow.

Tell about the activity you chose. What did you like about it?

_____

_____

_____

Parent's Signature _____

Mother's Day

Choose one activity. When it is completed, help your child dictate responses as you write them down at the bottom of the page. Return this page on the last school day of May.

1. Mother's Day Coupons

With someone other than Mom, have your child make a list of four helpful things to do for Mother's Day. Help your child fold a piece of paper into four sections and draw a picture of each idea in a section. Ask your child to cut the paper in fourths to make four "gift coupons" redeemable for the activities illustrated. Place the coupons in an envelope. Invite your child to decorate the envelope and tie a ribbon around it. Have your child present the envelope on Mother's Day to their mother or another special woman in their life.

2. Breakfast in Bed

Ask your child to assist the rest of the family (except for Mom) in making a special Mother's Day breakfast. Invite your child to measure, pour, and stir as breakfast is made.

Tell about the activity you chose. What did you like about it?

_____

_____

_____

Parent's Signature _____

Father's Day

Choose one activity. When it is completed, help your child dictate responses as you write them down at the bottom of the page. Return this page on the last school day of June.

1. Personalized Baseball Cap

Have your child practice drawing pictures that relate to his or her father on a piece of paper. Purchase a white baseball cap or a painter's cap, or use an old cap. Have your child use markers or fabric paints to copy the "practice" pictures on the cap. He or she can decorate a lunch bag and place the cap inside. Tie a ribbon around the top of the bag and have your child present it as a Father's Day gift.

2. Father's Day Play

Have your child and the rest of the family (except for Dad) choose a favorite story to act out as a Father's Day gift. Read the story, assign parts, design easy-to-make props, and practice the play before giving a terrific Father's Day performance.

Tell about the activity you chose. What did you like about it?

_____

_____

_____

Parent's Signature _____

Independence Day

Choose one activity. When it is completed, help your child dictate responses as you write them down at the bottom of the page. Return this page on the last school day of July.

1. Picnic Time

Help your child plan a pretend Fourth of July picnic. He or she can name all the people to invite. Then help your child make a list of picnic supplies such as food, paper products, and play equipment. Decide on a picnic location and time. Invite your child to design an invitation using markers, crayons, or a computer.

2. Fourth of July Decoration

As a family, discuss the significance of Independence Day. Have each family member tell why he or she feels fortunate to live in the United States. Invite your child to draw a picture of the reason that means the most to him or her. Display the picture as an Independence Day decoration.

Tell about the activity you chose. What did you like about it?

_____

_____

_____

Parent's Signature _____

Back to School

Choose one activity. When it is completed, help your child dictate responses as you write them down at the bottom of the page. Return this page on the last school day of August.

1. End of Summer Story

Help your child create a list of all the different activities he or she did during the summer. Ask which was his or her favorite activity. Write a story about this special time. When the story is complete, have your child draw a picture.

I went to the zoo.
I saw monkeys.
Watch them climb
from tree to tree.
I saw a giraffe
so, so tall, I wonder
if he saw me.

2. Fantasy Summer Story

Talk with your child about something he or she would have liked to have done during the summer. Discuss where this event happened, and the people involved. Write the story, and have your child draw a picture to go with it. Invite him or her to share the story with the rest of the family.

Tell about the activity you chose. What did you like about it?

_____

_____

_____

Parent's Signature _____

43   Creative Teaching Press, Inc.

Pick a Celebration

Choose one activity. When it is completed, record your child's response to the activity at the bottom of the page. Return this page on the last school day of the month.

1. Very Cool Video

Choose a favorite family tradition or celebration. Videotape the occasion and invite your child to be a commentator/narrator who gives a play-by-play description of the events. Watch the completed tape as a family after the celebration is over.

2. Plan a Party

Choose a favorite family celebration and invite your child to participate in the party planning. Help him or her make the invitations, choose the menu, make decorations, or take charge of entertainment such as games or performances.

Tell about the activity you chose. What did you like about it?

_____

_____

_____

Parent's Signature _____

Alphabet Fun

Alphabet Fun homework pages are designed to help children learn the alphabet. Each fun story features three or four letters of the alphabet.

As you teach these letters and sounds in the classroom, fill in the due date and duplicate the appropriate Letter Story to reinforce learning at home. The directions invite parents to read the story aloud as their children follow along. Activity choices follow the story. Each child is asked to complete at least three activities. Of course, many eager early learners will want to do them all! Ask them to return each Letter Story homework page on the due date.

Letter Story for S, T, and W

Return this Letter Story homework page by _____ .

1. Read the following story to your child as he or she follows along.

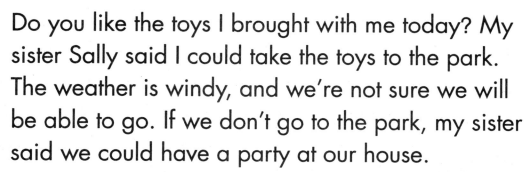

Do you like the toys I brought with me today? My sister Sally said I could take the toys to the park. The weather is windy, and we're not sure we will be able to go. If we don't go to the park, my sister said we could have a party at our house.

2. Have your child choose at least three of the following activities to complete. Check an activity box each time your child completes an activity.

☐ Circle all the capital and lowercase *Ss*, *Ts*, and *Ws* in the story.

☐ Say the sound each letter makes.

☐ Write each letter two times with your finger in sand or rice.

☐ Think of three other words that start with each letter.

☐ Cut out magazine pictures of objects that start with *S*, *T*, and *W*.

☐ Circle all the periods and question marks in the story.

Parent's Signature _____

Letter Story for M, P, and Z

Return this Letter Story homework page by _____ .

1. Read the following story to your child as he or she follows along.

My mother is taking us to the zoo today. My best friend, Pete, is going with my mom and me too! I can't wait to see the zebras and the monkeys. I wish I had a monkey for a pet, don't you?

2. Have your child choose at least three of the following activities to complete. Check an activity box each time your child completes an activity.

☐ Circle all the capital and lowercase Ms, Ps, and Zs in the story.

☐ Say the sound each letter makes.

☐ Write each letter two times with shaving cream or whipped cream.

☐ Think of three other words that start with each letter.

☐ While in the car, look out the window and find objects that start with M, P, and Z.

☐ Circle all the periods and question marks in the story.

Parent's Signature _____

Letter Story for A, D, and K

Return this Letter Story homework page by _____ .

1. Read the following story to your child as he or she follows along.

Alice and Danny have a new kitten. The kitten's name is Annie. She is dark brown. Danny told me to keep Annie on my lap while he cleans her kitty-litter box. Did you ever have a kitten? I have a dog, a bird, and a kitten.

2. Have your child choose at least three of the following activities to complete. Check an activity box each time your child completes an activity.
   - ☐ Circle all the capital and lowercase *A*s, *D*s, and *K*s in the story.
   - ☐ Say the sound each letter makes.
   - ☐ Write each letter two times with your finger in soapy water.
   - ☐ Think of three other words that start with each letter.
   - ☐ Open the refrigerator and name all the objects that start with *A*, *D*, and *K*.
   - ☐ Circle all the periods and question marks in the story.

Parent's Signature _____

Letter Story for G, N, X, and Y

Return this Letter Story homework page by _____ .

1. Read the following story to your child as he or she follows along.

My brother Nick gave me a yellow box. He said there was a surprise in it for me. I opened the box and found a gold necklace inside! I am so excited to have this necklace. I will wear it everywhere I go.

2. Have your child choose at least three of the following activities to complete. Check an activity box each time your child completes an activity.

☐ Circle all the capital and lowercase Gs, Ns, Xs, and Ys in the story.
☐ Say the sound each letter makes.
☐ Write each letter two times with a stick in the dirt.
☐ Think of three other words that have each letter.
☐ Look at the newspaper and point to pictures of objects that have each letter.
☐ Circle all the periods and question marks in the story.

Parent's Signature _____

Letter Story for B, F, R, and U

Return this Letter Story homework page by _____.

1. Read the following story to your child as he or she follows along.

Brad and Freddie are going to the fair on Friday. They asked me if I could go with them. I think it might rain, so I will take my umbrella. We can run into a building to keep dry. I bet we'll end up playing in the mud, don't you?

2. Have your child choose at least three of the following activities to complete. Check an activity box each time your child completes an activity.

☐ Circle all the capital and lowercase *B*s, *F*s, *R*s, and *U*s in the story.

☐ Say the sound each letter makes.

☐ Write each letter two times with your finger on a steamy mirror or window.

☐ Think of three other words that have each letter.

☐ Open your drawers and find clothing tags with words that have *B*, *F*, *R*, and *U*.

☐ Circle all the periods and question marks in the story.

Parent's Signature _____

Letter Story for C, I, and L

Return this Letter Story homework page by _____

1. Read the following story to your child as he or she follows along.

I love Lilly. She is my best friend. Lilly and I climbed a big hill. At the top of the hill Lilly gave me sixteen large lollipops! I love candy and so does Lilly. We licked until our tongues hurt. How many lollipops do you think we could eat?

2. Have your child choose at least three of the following activities to complete. Check an activity box each time your child completes an activity.

   ☐ Circle all the capital and lowercase Cs, Is, and Ls in the story.
   ☐ Say the sound each letter makes.
   ☐ Write each letter two times with your finger in a plate of rice.
   ☐ Think of three other words that have each letter.
   ☐ Open your kitchen cupboards and find foods that start with C, I, and L.
   ☐ Circle all the periods and question marks in the story.

Parent's Signature _____

Letter Story for E, H, and Q

Return this Letter Story homework page by _____ .

1. Read the following story to your child as he or she follows along.

While I was quietly sleeping, I heard three quacks coming from outside my window. I jumped out of bed and hurried to see where the sound was coming from. To my surprise, there were three ducks and two quail out in my yard! I crawled back into my bed, pulled my quilt over my head, and went back to sleep.

2. Have your child choose at least three of the following activities to complete. Check an activity box each time your child completes an activity.

☐ Circle all the lowercase *E*s, *H*s, and *Q*s in the story.
☐ Say the sound each letter makes.
☐ Write each letter two times with your finger on your palm.
☐ Think of three other words that have each letter.
☐ Look through a catalog and find objects that start with *E*, *H*, and *Q*.
☐ Circle all the periods and question marks in the story.

Parent's Signature _____

Name _____

Letter Story for J, O, and V

Return this Letter Story homework page by _____ .

1. Read the following story to your child as he or she follows along.

I have a very important job to do today. It's my mom's birthday and I am going to vacuum the house. Then I'm going to give her some pretty flowers. I will put the flowers in a vase. She will jump for joy when she sees what I did.

2. Have your child choose at least three of the following activities to complete. Check an activity box each time your child completes an activity.

☐ Circle all the capital and lowercase Js, Os, and Vs in the story.

☐ Say the sound each letter makes.

☐ Write each letter two times using pieces of cereal.

☐ Think of three other words that have each letter.

☐ Look through a photo album and point to all the things that start with J, O, and V.

☐ Circle all the periods and question marks in the story.

Parent's Signature _____

All the Letters Story

Return this Letter Story homework page by _____.

1. Read the following story to your child as he or she follows along.

> Last night I had a very strange dream. An ox and a zebra were blowing bubbles and riding bikes. Then they were jumping over a cactus. The ox fell on the cactus and jumped into the sky. That's quite funny, don't you think?

2. Have your child choose at least three of the following activities to complete. Check an activity box each time your child completes an activity.

☐ Circle each letter of the alphabet once in the story.
☐ Say the sound each letter makes.
☐ Write each letter of the alphabet once on paper.
☐ Find each letter of the alphabet in a favorite book.
☐ Think of one word that begins with each letter.
☐ Look through a catalog to find an object that begins or ends with each letter of the alphabet.
☐ Circle all the periods and question marks in the story.

Parent's Signature _____

Across the Curriculum

Real-life learning by its very nature crosses the curriculum. Across the Curriculum homework pages are designed to reinforce classroom learning in language arts, math, science, art, music, and physical education. These activities offer children the opportunity to successfully follow each task through to completion, and to develop the problem-solving skills so important in everyday life.

Each Across the Curriculum page begins with a section informing parents of the purpose of the homework. Easy-to-implement directions follow. The activities utilize simple items found in most households.

Before duplicating the homework page, simply fill in the due date. Ask children to bring back each of the completed projects or homework pages by the date you have filled in.

Author, Author!

Help your child complete this assignment. Turn it in by _____.

When a child creates a book, he or she is learning

- that writing and reading are important and enjoyable.
- to express his or her own thoughts, feelings, and ideas.
- that illustrations support the story.

Activity

1. Read a picture book to your child. Discuss the story. Talk about books in general. Point out that most picture books have covers, words that read from left to right, pages that turn from right to left, and illustrations that help explain the story.

2. Tell your child he or she is going to be the author of a story. Have him or her think of a story idea. For example, your child could write about a favorite experience or an imaginary friend.

3. Use several pieces of blank paper and invite your child to dictate the story while you write it word for word. Write the story at the bottom of each page in order to leave room for illustrations.

4. Have your child illustrate each book page.

5. Stack the pages and place blank paper on the top and bottom of the stack for covers. Write the title on the front cover. Have your child draw a cover illustration.

6. To bind the book, staple the pages or punch holes in the left side of the stack and tie yarn, ribbon, or shoelaces through the holes.

7. Invite your child to read the completed book to the family.

8. Send the completed book to school.

Parent's Signature _____

Now Hear This!

Help your child complete this assignment. Turn it in by _____.

When a child practices listening, he or she is learning

- how to follow directions.
- to concentrate and pay attention.
- complex language patterns for use in his or her own speech.

Activity

Play these listening games with your child for great listening practice. There are three levels: easy, intermediate, and advanced. Try one, two, or all three.

- **Easy:** Perform a simple "body-sound" pattern such as *clap, clap, clap* or *clap, snap, clap, snap*. Have your child repeat it. Invite your child to repeat several different patterns until he or she can mimic them with ease.

- **Intermediate:** Give your child two or more verbal directions in a row, such as *Touch your nose and then your head*. Have your child perform the actions. Advance to more complicated instructions such as *touch your head twice, then turn around*. Invite your child to perform the actions until he or she can easily follow your directions.

- **Advanced:** Say several words in a specific order. Have your child repeat the words you say in the same order. Examples could include *Two, four, six, eight; Hop, jump, sit, stand;* or *Susie saw a sandwich on the seashore*.

Tell about the activity you chose. What did you like about it?

_____

_____

_____

Parent's Signature _____

Family Captions

Help your child complete this assignment. Turn it in by _____.

When your child creates captions for photos or illustrations, he or she is learning
- that writing is enjoyable.
- that letters on a page represent words and ideas.
- to express his or her own thoughts, feelings, and ideas.

Activity

1. Invite your child to study a family photograph. (Your child can draw an illustration of the family if a photo is not available.)
2. Ask your child to dictate a sentence for each family member to say or think.
3. Write each sentence, word for word, on separate "sticky notes" or small pieces of paper. Have your child cut around the sentences to make "speech bubbles." Ask him or her to tape the speech bubbles to the photograph or illustration.
4. Invite your child to display the photo or illustration and read the captions to the family.
5. Send the completed photo or illustration to school.

Parent's Signature _____

Color Walk

Help your child complete this assignment. Turn it in by _____.

When your child identifies colors, he or she can learn

- word meaning.
- that colors are used to draw people's attention to things.
- to develop thoughts and ideas about colors.

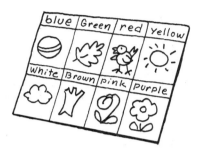

Activity

1. Go on a walk with your child. Have him or her identify different objects that are red, blue, green, brown, orange, white, black, yellow, and purple.

2. Back at home, have your child draw a picture of one thing for each color that he or she saw. Draw each picture in a box below.

3. Help your child write each color above the picture, or write the word for your child.

_____	_____	_____	_____
_____	_____	_____	_____

Parent's Signature _____

All About Me!

Help your child complete this assignment. Turn it in by _____.

When your child memorizes personal information, he or she is learning

- word meaning.
- how to respond verbally to questions.
- important safety information.

My last name is Martinez.

Activity

1. Read the following statements with your child and review the correct answers.
2. Write the correct answers on the lines.
3. Read the answers to your child, pointing to each word as you say it.
4. Help your child memorize the information.
5. Review the statements frequently over several days until your child can recite them without your help.

My first name is _____.

My last name is _____.

My address is _____

_____

My telephone number is _____.

The number to call in an emergency is _____.

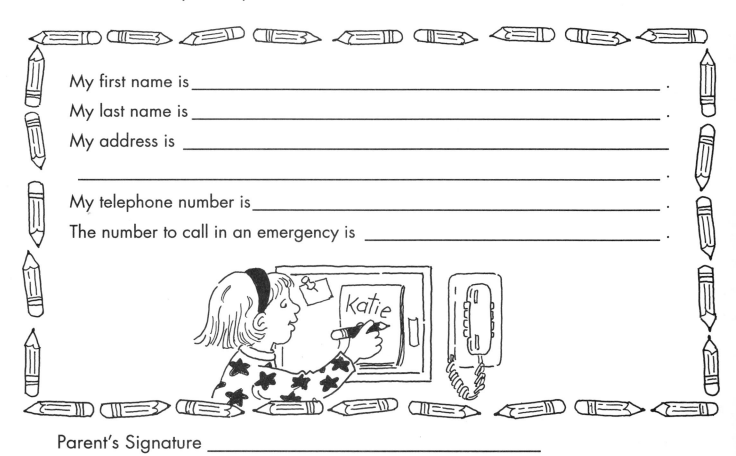

Parent's Signature _____

Design a Castle!

Help your child complete this assignment. Turn it in by _____.

When your child listens to fairy tales, he or she is learning

- that reading is important and enjoyable.
- to use his or her imagination.
- to recognize words in print.

Activity

1. Read your child several fairy tales that tell about castles such as *Cinderella, Sleeping Beauty, Rapunzel,* or *Rumpelstiltskin.*

2. Discuss the stories and especially the castles. Ask your child to imagine the rooms mentioned in the stories and describe them.

3. Invite your child to be the "head architect" who directs family members in drawing a castle on either poster board or blank pieces of paper taped together. Have your child participate in the drawing as well.

4. Label each room on the drawing as your child names it.

Parent's Signature _____

Name Game

Help your child complete this assignment. Turn it in by _____.

When your child works with rhyming words, he or she is learning
* to hear sounds in words (phonemic awareness).
* that letters have specific sounds.
* that words are made of letter/sound combinations.

Activity

1. Read aloud a favorite nursery rhyme or rhyming poem.
2. Invite your child to listen for words that rhyme.
3. Point to the rhyming words and say them aloud. Invite your child to say them after you.
4. Select one pair of rhyming words from the nursery rhyme, such as *Jill* and *hill*. Encourage your child to think of another word that rhymes with those words, such as *fill*. Accept all rhyming words even if they are nonsense words.
5. Help your child write the pairs of rhyming words on the lines below.

pair 1 _____   _____

pair 2 _____   _____

pair 3 _____   _____

pair 4 _____   _____

pair 5 _____   _____

Jack

Jill

Parent's Signature _____

Sorting of All Sorts

Help your child complete this assignment. Turn it in by _____.

When your child sorts objects, he or she is learning

- to identify similarities and differences.
- to place objects in identifiable categories.
- the concepts of color, size, and shape.

Activity

1. Have your child collect at least 20 small objects of the same kind, such as an assortment of candies, buttons, or coins.

2. Ask your child to sort the objects by color. Invite your child to explain why he or she put the objects in each category.

3. Invite your child to sort the objects by size. Again, have your child explain why he or she put the objects in each category.

4. Challenge your child to think of new ways to sort the items, such as by texture or by how they are used.

5. In the box below have your child draw one way he or she sorted the items.

Parent's Signature _____

63

Measure Up!

Help your child complete this assignment. Turn it in by _____.

When your child measures real-life objects, he or she is learning

- that two objects can be compared by size.
- numerical concepts of more and less.
- logical reasoning.

Activity

1. Measure a piece of string around your child's waist and cut it to size.

2. Invite your child to search the house and find three objects that are approximately the same length as the string. Help your child write the objects' names on the lines below.

3. Have your child find three objects that are longer than the string. Help him or her list these items.

4. Encourage your child to find three things that are shorter than the string. Help him or her list these items.

Same Length	**Longer**	**Shorter**
_____	_____	_____
_____	_____	_____
_____	_____	_____
_____	_____	_____

Parent's Signature _____

Order Up!

Help your child complete this assignment. Turn it in by _____.

When your child works with ordinal numbers, he or she is learning

- sequencing skills.
- that objects can be compared by location.
- the concepts of before, between, and after.

Activity

1. Write the words *first, second, third, fourth,* and *fifth* on separate index cards or pieces of paper.

2. Place the cards in order on a table.

3. Invite your child to line up five stuffed animals or toys next to the cards.

4. Have your child tell what "place" the animals or toys are in by saying the ordinal number that goes with each object. For example, your child might say, *The bear is first, the pelican is second, the tiger is third*, and so on.

5. Mix up the cards but leave the objects in the same order.

6. Point to the first object.

7. Help your child find the card that says *first*, and move it next to the first object. Repeat the activity with each object.

8. Invite your child to draw each object in the correct box below.

first	**second**	**third**	**fourth**	**fifth**

Parent's Signature _____

1 to 20, Numbers A-Plenty!

Help your child complete this assignment. Turn it in by _____.

When your child works with number symbols, he or she is learning
- that written symbols represent numbers or tangible objects.
- that numbers follow a logical order.
- that number symbols have similarities and differences.

Activity

1. Help your child write the numbers from 1 to 20 in the squares below. Number across.
2. Have your child say each number as he or she writes it in a square.
3. Name the numbers out of order, and have your child circle each number as you say it.

Parent's Signature _____

Counting Treasures

Help your child complete this assignment. Turn it in by _____.

When your child counts real-life objects, he or she is learning

- that numbers can represent tangible objects.
- that numbers have meaning.
- concepts of more and less.

Activity

1. Place at least 20 "treasures" in a plastic bag. Treasures could include candies, buttons, crayons, nuts, and toothpicks.

2. Randomly call out a number from 1 to 10.

3. Have your child count out that many objects and lay them on a table.

4. Ask your child to write the number on a piece of paper.

5. Put the objects back in the bag and repeat the activity until all ten numbers have been written.

6. Invite your child to draw a picture of ten items and write the number 10 on the back of this paper.

Parent's Signature _____

Pick a Pattern

Help your child complete this assignment. Turn it in by _____ .

When your child makes patterns, he or she is learning

- to see patterns in the real world.
- to recognize patterns in numbers.
- logical reasoning.

Activity

1. Gather groups of small household objects such as toothpicks, paper clips, rubber bands, pennies, and dimes.
2. Sort the objects into piles.
3. Invite your child to arrange objects to form a pattern, repeating the pattern at least two times.
4. Challenge him or her to make at least two other patterns from the objects.
5. Have your child draw one of the patterns on the back of this paper.

Parent's Signature _____

How Much Will It Hold?

Help your child complete this assignment. Turn it in by _____.

When your child estimates, he or she is learning
- to approximate numbers.
- logical reasoning.
- concepts of more and less.

Activity

1. Fill a clear jar with small objects of the same kind, such as marshmallows, jelly beans, oyster crackers, stones, pennies, or marbles.

2. Have everyone in the family estimate how many objects are in the jar. Write the estimates on a piece of paper.

3. Take the items out of the jar and divide them into groups of ten.

4. Help your child count by tens to find out how many items were in the jar.

5. Write the actual number of items below. Compare this number to the estimates.

6. Have your child tell whose estimation came the closest and whose was farthest off.

7. Have your child record the winner's information below.

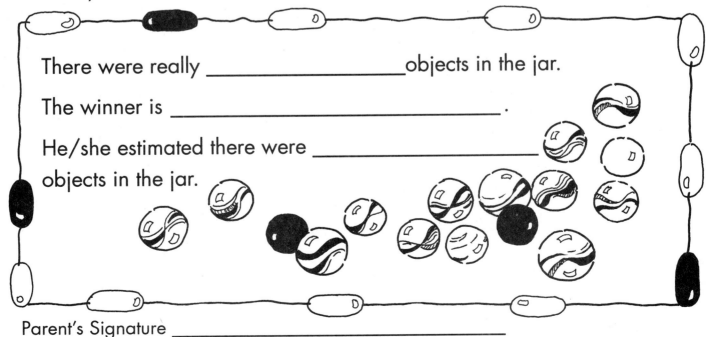

There were really _____ objects in the jar.

The winner is _____ .

He/she estimated there were _____ objects in the jar.

Parent's Signature _____

Sink or Float?

Help your child complete this assignment. Turn it in by _____.

When your child plays with water, he or she is learning
- that some things sink and some things float (density).
- concepts of empty and full.
- concept of volume.

Activity

1. Invite your child to gather at least 20 different objects that can get wet.
2. Fill a tub or sink with water.
3. Invite your child to place one object at a time in the water.
4. Discuss what happens as each object is placed in the water. Ask questions such as: *Did the object sink or float? Did water fill the object? How high did the water level rise?*
5. Ask your child whether there is air inside the object. Ask which is heavier, water or air.
6. Assist your child in writing the answers below.

List five things that floated.	**List five things that sank.**
_____	_____
_____	_____
_____	_____
_____	_____
_____	_____

Parent's Signature _____

Modeling Dough

Help your child complete this assignment. Turn it in by _____.

When your child makes homemade modeling dough, he or she is learning

- that matter changes states.
- concepts of wet and dry.
- that the amount of a substance remains the same, even when the shape changes (conservation).
- how to measure.

Activity

1. Under close adult supervision, have your child make the following recipe.

   Modeling Dough
   Combine in a saucepan: 4 cups flour, 2 cups salt, 4 tablespoons oil, 8 teaspoons cream of tartar, 4 cups water, and a desired amount of food coloring. Bring the mixture to a boil. Cook on low heat for 3–5 minutes. Remove from heat, cool, place on a floured board, and knead.

2. Invite your child to make several objects from the dough.
3. Allow one object to dry and send it to school. (The rest of the dough can be kept in a container with a lid.)

Parent's Signature _____

71

Beautiful Babies

Help your child complete this assignment. Turn it in by _____.

When your child discusses animal babies, he or she is learning
- that living things grow and change.
- that life follows a logical and predictable cycle.
- that living things reproduce.

Activity

1. Have your child observe the animal pictures below.
2. Together discuss how each animal comes into the world. (Reptiles hatch from eggs. Birds hatch from eggs. Mammals are born alive. Fish hatch from eggs. Insects hatch from eggs.)
3. Help your child write *egg* or *alive* under each of the animal pictures.
4. Invite him or her to draw a human baby in the last square.

Parent's Signature _____

Sidewalk Chalk

Help your child complete this assignment. Turn it in by _____.

When your child makes homemade sidewalk chalk, he or she is learning

- that matter changes states.
- the concepts of wet and dry.
- how to measure.

Activity

1. Under close adult supervision, help your child make the following recipe.

   Sidewalk Chalk
   Place one cup of Plaster of Paris into a mixing bowl. Stirring constantly, slowly add water until the plaster resembles pudding. Add tempera paint until the mixture is the desired color.

2. Have your child pour the plaster into several plastic cups and set the cups aside for about a day or until dry.

3. Ask your child to describe the changes that take place in the mixture.

4. When dry, turn the cups upside down, and then hit them on a hard surface until the chalk pops out. Take the chalk outside and have fun.

5. Invite your child to draw one picture with the chalk on the back of this page.

Parent's Signature _____

Planting Time

Help your child complete this assignment. Turn it in by _____.

When your child plants an indoor garden, he or she is learning

- that the earth gives plants nutrients (food) to survive.
- parts of a plant.
- that plants need water and sunlight to survive.
- that living things grow and change.

Activity

1. Take your child to the garden section of a store, and invite him or her to choose flower or herb seeds to plant indoors. (Radishes are fast and easy to grow.)
2. Have your child plant the seeds in soil in individual pots.
3. Ask him or her to place the pots in a sunny location.
4. Have your child water the plants approximately every other day.
5. Invite him or her to observe the plants every day for signs of growth.
6. Assist your child in completing the statements at the bottom of this page.

I planted _____.

I gave the plant _____ so it could grow.

This is how my plant looks. (Draw a picture of the plant as changes occur.)

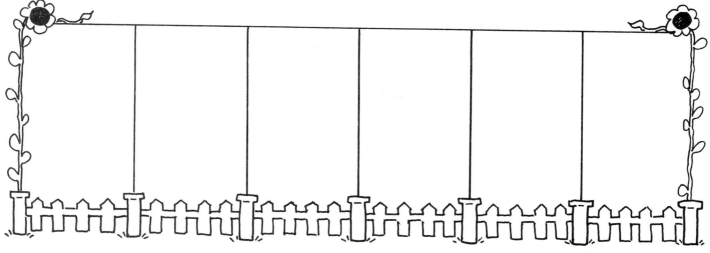

Parent's Signature _____

Finger Jell-O

Help your child complete this assignment. Turn it in by _____.

When your child makes food, he or she is learning
- how heat and cold change things.
- concepts of volume and measurement.
- that matter changes states.

Activity

1. Under close adult supervision, have your child make the following recipe.

Finger Jello
Combine four small packages of Jell-O gelatin and $2\frac{1}{2}$ cups boiling water. Stir until the gelatin is dissolved. Pour the mixture into a 9" x 13" pan. Chill at least three hours.

2. Invite your child to cut shapes in the Jell-O with cookie cutters. Eat and enjoy!
3. Help your child answer the following questions.

What did the Jell-O look like when it first came out of the package? _____

_____

How did the hot water change the Jell-O? _____

_____

How did chilling the Jell-O change it? _____

_____

Parent's Signature _____

Music Makers

Help your child complete this assignment. Turn it in by _____.

When your child uses rhythm instruments, he or she is learning

- to be conscious of rhythm and tempo in music.
- concepts of fast, slow, loud, and soft.
- listening skills.

Activity

1. Have your child make simple rhythm instruments by using:
   - a pot top and wooden spoon
   - two sticks
   - an empty shoe box (minus the lid) with a rubber band stretched over it
   - a glass of water and a spoon
2. Make an instrument for yourself.
3. Play music with a slow tempo on the radio.
4. Invite your child to play the instrument to the beat of the music.
5. Play fast music and have him or her repeat the activity.
6. Play other games with the instruments such as playing loudly and softly, making up your own rhythms, or having your child repeat a rhythm after you.
7. On the back of this paper have your child draw the instrument he or she used.

Parent's Signature _____

Name That Tune

Help your child complete this assignment. Turn it in by _____.

When your child listens to and sings songs, he or she is learning

- to be conscious of rhythm in music.
- the concept of tone and pitch.
- auditory discrimination (recognizing differences in sounds).

Activity

1. Play a simplified version of "Name That Tune" with your child. Think of a familiar tune such as "Twinkle, Twinkle, Little Star."
2. Hum the first three notes of the song, and challenge your child to guess the name of the song.
3. Add more notes until your child recognizes the song. Start at the beginning of the song each time you add more notes.
4. Invite your child to hum three notes of a song for you. (Have another family member help your child if necessary.)
5. Play the game several times.
6. Ask your child the questions below. Write the answers for him or her.

   What was the hardest part of this game? _____

   _____

   What part of this game was the most fun? _____

   _____

Parent's Signature _____

77

Animal Collage

Help your child complete this assignment. Turn it in by _____.

When your child makes a collage, he or she is learning

- to exercise imagination and creativity.
- concepts of shape, size, location, and design.
- how to create patterns and designs.

Activity

1. Gather several different magazines.
2. Have your child cut out pictures of his or her favorite animals.
3. Using a large piece of paper or cardboard, have your child arrange the pictures in overlapping positions until he or she decides each picture is in the best place.
4. Have your child glue the pictures onto the paper to make a collage.
5. Send the collage to school.

Parent's Signature _____

Finger Paint Pudding

Help your child complete this assignment. Turn it in by _____.

When your child finger paints, he or she is learning

- to exercise imagination and creativity.
- hand-eye coordination.
- to have fun sharing ideas with others.

Activity

1. Make chocolate or vanilla instant pudding according to the directions on the box.
2. Use the pudding as paint to make a design on large paper. Show your child how to use a fingernail, a fist, and individual fingers to make patterns. Encourage your child to be creative.
3. Don't forget to lick your fingers when you're finished! Yum!
4. Because the art work will not thoroughly dry, do not send it to school. Instead, have your child write several sentences on the back of this paper telling how he or she created the finger painting.

Parent's Signature _____

Puzzles

Help your child complete this assignment. Turn it in by _____.

When your child makes and plays with a puzzle, he or she is learning

- about the relationships of parts to the whole.
- hand-eye coordination.
- concepts of shapes, size, color and location.
- problem-solving skills.
- about negative and positive space
  (seeing something against its background).

Activity

1. Have your child put a "store-bought" puzzle together so he or she has an understanding of how puzzles work.
2. Invite your child to find a favorite picture in a magazine and carefully tear it out.
3. Trim a blank sheet of paper to match the size of the picture. The paper will later serve as a guide.
4. Have your child draw puzzle-piece cutting lines across the picture.
5. Assist your child in cutting out the pieces.
6. Have your child put the puzzle together on the blank piece of paper.
7. Send the puzzle to school in an envelope or resealable plastic bag.

Parent's Signature _____

Jump-a-Rhyme

Help your child complete this assignment. Turn it in by _____.

When your child jumps rope to rhymes, he or she is learning

- to develop large motor skills.
- principles of music and rhythm.
- memory skills and sequencing.

Activity

1. Obtain a jump rope or clothesline. Choose one of the following jump-rope methods to teach your child.

   - Place the rope on the floor. Have your child jump back and forth over the still rope.
   - Tie the rope to a doorknob and swing it back and forth at ankle level (not overhead). Have your child jump the rope.
   - Tie the rope to a doorknob and swing the rope overhead. Have your child jump the rope.

2. Use one of the jump-rope rhymes below or one of your own as your child jumps.

3. Invite your child to draw a picture of himself or herself jumping rope on the back of this page.

Cinderella dressed in yellow
Went upstairs to kiss a fellow.
Made a mistake and kissed a snake.
How many doctors did it take?
One, two, three, four, five . . .
(Continue counting until your child misses.)

Teddy bear, teddy bear,
Turn around.
Teddy bear, teddy bear,
Touch the ground.
Teddy bear, teddy bear,
Turn out the light.
Teddy bear, teddy bear,
Say Goodnight.

Parent's Signature _____

81

Name _____

Scissor Shapes

Help your child complete this assignment. Turn it in by _____.

When your child uses scissors, he or she is learning
- to control the small muscles of his or her hand.
- concepts of shape, size, and location.
- hand-eye coordination.

Activity

1. Draw a large rectangle, heart, circle, and wavy line on separate pieces of paper so each drawing fills most of the paper.
2. Give your child each paper and invite him or her to use scissors and cut on the lines.
3. Place the shapes in an envelope and send them to school.

Parent's Signature _____

Family Adventures

A trip to the grocery store . . . or a trip to Mars? Family Adventure homework pages invite students and their families to go on real-life or make-believe adventures together. And naturally, families learn as they go! These real-life experiences will develop creative and critical thinking skills as well as enhance learning in social studies, reading, writing, and science.

Fill in the due date at the top of the Family Adventure page, and duplicate it. Then discuss the page together, and send it home. Each homework page begins with an adventure idea. There is always the possibility to turn a real-life adventure into a make-believe one if the family is unable to go by saying: "Let's pretend we went to . . ."

A list of activity suggestions follows each adventure idea. The directions invite families to discuss and choose together at least three activities to complete. They can check the box in front of the activity description and then return the page by the due date.

The Grocery Store Adventure

Help your child complete this assignment. Turn it in by _____ .

Load the family in the car and take a trip to the grocery store! Make a stop at the produce section, and help your child complete and check off at least three of the following activities. Return this list by the due date.

- ☐ Find at least two fruits and vegetables that are grown in your state.
- ☐ Point to five fruits and five vegetables.
- ☐ Buy one thing your family has never tasted before.
- ☐ Name all the different colors you see.
- ☐ Weigh a potato and a tomato on the produce scale. Which one weighs more? Which one weighs less?
- ☐ Read five signs or have someone read them to you.
- ☐ Back at home, draw a picture using as many fruits and vegetables as you can.

Parent's Signature _____

Trip to Mars Adventure

Pretend your family is going on a space mission to Mars. Help your child complete at least three of the following activities. Return this list by _____.

☐ Make a list of all the supplies you will need to take with you for food, shelter, and safety. Attach the list to this paper.

☐ Use blankets, furniture, and other household objects to create your family's spaceship. Don't forget to add a room for the pilot, a laboratory for experiments, and a room for living.

☐ Trips into space are science missions. What experiment might you perform in space? Perform a similar experiment in the kitchen.

☐ Name five things you expect to see in space.

☐ Name three things you expect to hear in space. Try to imitate the sounds.

☐ If there are other life-forms on Mars, what might they look like? Draw a picture. Attach it to this paper.

Parent's Signature _____

Vacation Adventure

Plan a real or make-believe vacation as a family. Help your child complete at least three of the following activities as you make the plans and take the trip. Return this list by _____.

☐ Mark on the map where you are starting and where you will be going.

☐ During a car trip, look for license plates from different states that you will pass through on your trip.

☐ Look in the newspaper to find out what the weather is like in the place where you are going.

☐ Look at a map or an atlas to find out how long it will take you to get to your destination by car.

☐ Make a list of everything you need to pack.

☐ List the places where you might stop along the way such as restaurants, gas stations, and rest stops.

☐ Think of three places you hope to visit on the way and tell what you expect to find there.

☐ Before you go, write down what you think you will like most and least about the trip.

☐ Write at least three entries in a journal about your trip.

Parent's Signature _____

Picnic at the Park Adventure

Go on a family picnic to a nearby park. Help your child complete at least three of the following activities before, during, and after the trip. Return this list by
_____.

- ☐ Make a list of everything you will need to take.
- ☐ Look at a map and point out how to get to the park.
- ☐ Estimate how long it will take for you to get there.
- ☐ Name the different types of transportation you can use to get there.
- ☐ Name five activities your family can participate in when you get to the park.
- ☐ Count on your fingers the number of people going with you.
- ☐ Once at the park, take a walk and challenge family members to name at least three different types of trees and plants.
- ☐ Name all the types of play equipment at the park and tell your favorite ones to play on.
- ☐ Name all the animals you see at the park.
- ☐ Pick grass. When you get home make a picture using the grass blades.
- ☐ Count and tell the number of people you remember seeing at the park.

Parent's Signature _____

Neighborhood Adventure

Take a family walk around your backyard and neighborhood. Then complete at least three of the following activities as a family. Have fun! Return this list by _____.

- ☐ Count all the birds you see.
- ☐ Name other animals you see.
- ☐ Tell five sounds you hear.
- ☐ Guess where different smells are coming from and what they are.
- ☐ Lift up a rock or branch lying on the ground. Do you see any insects?
- ☐ Name five objects and tell their colors.
- ☐ Find things that are made out of wood, plastic, cement, rock, and metal.
- ☐ Find things that are smooth, rough, and prickly.
- ☐ Talk about how the weather feels (windy, hot, cold, wet).
- ☐ Read all the signs you see.
- ☐ Read the numbers on the houses and buildings.
- ☐ When you return home, draw a picture about your adventure.

Parent's Signature _____

Name _____

Camping Adventure

Plan and go on a real or make-believe camping trip. Then complete at least three of the following activities as a family. Return this list by_____.

- ☐ Make a list of all the supplies you will need to take with you.
- ☐ Categorize the items on the list as food, clothing, camping gear, or entertainment.
- ☐ Name three games you want to take along.
- ☐ When you are there, take a nature walk. What do you see, smell, and hear?
- ☐ Read the signs you see. Which ones are for safety and which ones are for directions?
- ☐ Name five animals you see.
- ☐ Describe the different kinds of trees and bushes you see.
- ☐ Make a list of all the things that are different about camping and staying at a hotel.
- ☐ Tell someone what you like best about camping. Tell someone what you like least about camping.
- ☐ Imagine you had a special camper or tent. What would it look like? What would it have inside and outside? Draw and label the camper or tent.

Parent's Signature _____

Imaginary City Adventure

As a family, plan a trip to an imaginary city. Then complete at least three of the following activities with your child. Return this list by_____.

- ☐ Think of a name for your city.
- ☐ Think of all the ways you can get there.
- ☐ Draw a picture of what you want the city to look like.
- ☐ Tell someone how people travel there. Do they go by cars or spaceships? What other vehicles will people use?
- ☐ Make a list of stores found in the city.
- ☐ Pretend you are taking a walk in your city. Tell what you see.
- ☐ Name the ways this city is different from your own neighborhood.
- ☐ Draw a picture of the animals found there.
- ☐ What do people do for fun? Tell someone.
- ☐ Create a sports team. What do they play and what is their name?
- ☐ Use your toys or boxes and crayons and make a model of the imaginary city.

Parent's Signature _____

Timely Tips Newsletters

Timely Tips Newsletters are perfect mediums for conveying important information to parents on such topics as homework, reading, television, and self-confidence. Parents want to be good partners in their child's education, but often lack the knowledge or confidence to deal with these issues in an effective way.

Share and discuss these Timely Tips Newsletters with parents at an open house or send them home with students at appropriate times throughout the year. You will find that parents will appreciate this valuable support/assistance.

 # Homework

Timely Tips Newsletter

Did You Know?

Homework can turn into "homeplay" when you support your child and do your best to make learning at home a fun experience. Use the following tips to help your child make the most of homework experiences.

- Set a regular time and place to do the homework. Allow your child to help make this decision so she or he is part of the decision-making process.

- Help your child find a quiet and comfortable place to work. Encourage him or her to avoid interruptions. Turn off the TV.

- Provide the necessary tools such as paper, pencils, crayons, and scissors.

- When necessary, read the directions to your child and make sure they are understood.

- If necessary, demonstrate how to complete the homework before having your child try it alone.

- Whenever appropriate, sign your child's homework paper. This sends a message to the teacher that you are involved in your child's learning.

- If you have any questions regarding assignments, ask the teacher.

- Praise your child's efforts and keep the atmosphere positive.

Reading

Timely Tips Newsletter

Did You Know?

Your child will become a better learner when you are his or her partner in education. As one of the most important people in your child's life, you have an opportunity to make a critical difference in how successful your child will be in school. Reading together is one way to become your child's partner in education. Use the following tips when reading with your child.

- Read to your child every night if you can. It is one of the most important activities the two of you can share. Use the time to cuddle up together and make the reading experience loving and enjoyable.

- Remember not to turn every reading session into a lesson. Your overall goal is to provide a pleasurable reading experience.

- Choose books that are the appropriate level for your child.

- Choose books that are of interest to your child.

- Occasionally, have your child place his or her finger under each word as the two of you read.

- Ask your child to predict what will happen next at a natural point in a story.

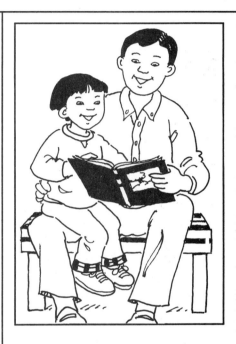

- Ask your child if he or she liked the way the book ended. If not, ask how he or she might change it.

- Children often choose to read or listen to the same books over and over. Go for it! This repetition helps your child with vocabulary, word recognition, and story sequence, among other important skills.

- Don't worry about having your child read to you. Your child will gain more from the experience if he or she is allowed to listen and take in the story while you read.

               Creative Teaching Press, Inc.

 # Television

Timely Tips Newsletter

Did You Know?

As every parent knows, television can interfere with and delay the completion of homework. Use the following techniques to make television-viewing a more meaningful experience for your child.

- Set limits. Establish good habits by allowing your child to view TV for only an hour (or less) a day.

- Plan. Look at your local television guide and decide together which shows to watch. Talk about which ones are appropriate and at what times they should be viewed.

- Participate. Watch together the shows you choose. Discuss parts of the show and explain things when necessary. Ask your child for ideas about ways the show could have been presented differently.

- Monitor. Encourage your child to choose programs about positive and loving situations. Discuss the characters and why they do what they do.

- Analyze commercials. Help your child analyze commercials and recognize exaggerated claims.

- Seek alternatives. Instead of watching television, have your child participate in activities such as music lessons; after-school sports, programs or clubs; or at-home arts and crafts projects.

Learning on the Go

Timely Tips Newsletter

Did You Know?

The "real world" is the most natural place for your child to learn. It abounds with new and exciting educational experiences. Invite your child to learn in the real world by participating with you in some of the following activities.

- Visit community buildings and attractions such as a farm, museum, or fire station.

- Take your child on errands to the grocery store, cleaners, post office, and hardware store. Take time to browse around and talk about the different jobs people have.

- Provide free or unstructured time for your child. Invite him or her to listen to music, daydream, or learn to entertain him- or herself.

- Take a train trip or a bus ride.

- Have your child obtain a library card and visit the library regularly. Set a good example for your child by checking out books for yourself as well.

- Take walks in your neighborhood.

- Go to special events such as sporting events, concerts, or movies. Try to find events that are free and age-appropriate.

- Have your child join community organizations such as the Scouts, 4-H Club, Camp Fire, soccer, or T-ball programs.

- Play a board game or do a puzzle together.

- Read signs, license plates, bumper stickers, and billboards together.

- Talk about the environment such as the colors, smells, and noises around you.

- When in the car, talk about directions, traffic rules, and what to expect next.

Building Your Child's ♡ Self-Confidence ♡

Timely Tips Newsletter

- Display your child's creations such as drawings, paintings, and writings.

- Photograph your child engaged in a learning task and display the photos around the house.

- Encourage your child in a positive way to try again when he or she is unsuccessful or frustrated.

- Spend time together. Work, play, talk, or just be together for a little while every day.

- Through words and hugs, let your child know that you believe in him or her.

- Remind your child that it is "okay" to make mistakes.

Did You Know?

With support and guidance, every child can learn. And you can provide that support by working to build your child's self-confidence in learning. Use the following tips to help your child develop self-esteem and self-confidence.

- Praise your child every time you see something positive. Be specific about your praise by telling him or her what you like and why.

- Set realistic goals for your child.

- Be patient with your child when he or she tries something new. Remind your child that "practice makes perfect."

- Let your child learn things on his or her own whenever possible. Children spend a lot of time trying to make sense of their world.